MW00577323

The Art of Bars: Twelve Steps in the War Against the Self

poems by

Mickey J. Corrigan

Finishing Line Press
Georgetown, Kentucky

The Art of Bars: Twelve Steps in the War Against the Self

ACKNOWLEDGMENTS

Poems have appeared or will appear in the following publications:
R.kv.r.y Quarterly Literary Journal
Transcendental Visions
Penny Ante Feud

Gracias to Cap'n Sass for the soup, sangria, and sage input on all of these poems.

Thank you to Elizabeth Aronson for her all-in support.

Publisher: Leah Maines

Editor: Christen Kincaid

Cover Art: Samuel P. Hughes

Author Photo: Mel H. Goss

Cover Design: Mel Goss

Printed in the USA on acid-free paper.
Order online: www.finishinglinepress.com
            also available on amazon.com

Author inquiries and mail orders:
Finishing Line Press
P. O. Box 1626
Georgetown, Kentucky 40324
U. S. A.

Table of Contents/Steps

Never leave an enemy behind
or it will rise again to fly at your throat.

—Shaka Zulu

"The greatest victory is that which requires no battle."

—Sun Tzu, The Art of War

To Avoid Defeat

On the way to the gym, neon
beckons you in. *Just one,*
and you're done.
That Irish salute.

The soft hum, coolness
refreshing those inherited cells
your DNA calling you out,
Celtic ancestors in formation,
their whiskey, beer, hard comforts.

You quit being that
version of you
every morning,
only to start again
each night. *Here's how*
and here you are

a woman
drinking
alone.
Hair back.
Nails bitten.
Bike shorts skin tight,
too short. Too short
for what?

Not for whatever
you have in mind
for now.

Thinking deep thoughts
depresses you.
Wading thigh high
in the shallows
uplifts.

Know the enemy and
know the self.
In a hundred battles
you will not be
defeated.
In a hundred bars
choose cunning over force
and you will stumble out
alive.

Your own shadow
more company than you
might like, ask yourself this:
How did you decide
to abandon
your life?
And, in what order?

Hard to watch
the vivid pornography
of your own downslide?
Go ahead and guzzle,
thirsty for the other, thirsty
for something, someone
to slake you
to make you last.

The darkness lures you in, soothing
with a hard hand that takes.
Ignore that man on the next stool
ignore his warm touch,
his random eyes and
the secret dark hole
unspoken and shared.

Nothing to lose means nothing.

Yourself, in battle;
in bars:
fucked up
fucked often
whatever the fuck,
then—

nothing.

The Unexpected You

Lift the drink
to your pinked, plumped lips.
Dive in and slip
beneath the surface.

Above you
the world:
muted, distant, safe.

Close your tired eyes,
drink alone.
Drink more.

Attack the enemy
where it waits, most
unprepared.
Act when you are most
unexpected.
Go for the throat
and choke yourself off.
Seize
the element of surprise.
Become
the embodiment of another:
not you.

Drunk: a way to make him look
like the man you always wanted.

Drunk: the best you can expect
from your irrepressible dark side.

The chaos of Eros.
Thanatos. Booze.
The enveloping listlessness
of your headspun disillusion.

The propulsive happiness
of self-infliction, the fantasy
of not being alone.

Bottoms up.

Reflected in that liquid,
glass, mirror
behind the bar:
a woman, drinking.
                    The enemy, waiting.

Excellence in Policy

To subdue the enemy
without fighting—this is
the supreme excellence.
Your head tonight
full of such policy. War-fogged,
aroused but with historic
intentions.

Today the sun glistened
on tender green leaves.
The sky hung low
blissful, clean.
You felt like shit.

                Ever notice
Monet only looks good at
twenty-five feet away?
                Your brain
a hotel lobby full of guests;
none stay.
                You said
you have no power
over your rubbery limbs, voice,
self. Another round?
                Free
to make conventional choices,
to self-destruct.
This feels better
than that.

Your marriage a boot camp,
then you went to war.
No worshipper
of subordination
you remained engaged.
Now peace at home
a squalid paradise of emptiness.

Drinking alone. A woman like you.

Drinking alone with you. A man
like all the other men
you lure home
fuck and forget.
Regret.

When you are angry at yourself:
who is it you are angry with?
So you stranger fuck, so what?

Declare a truce with that side
of yourself.
Go ahead.
Drink to it.

A Sleight of Hand

All warfare is based on this:
deception. Tonight, your mask
alcohol and brass and disarray
to hide your self-impersonation.

Mahogany bar, sports on twelve
flat screen TVs.
Happy hour cheese
hard to the touch.
Tiny cold
hot dogs on sticks.
Drunks laughing,
your face
unreadable,
gaping mouth socked,
duct-taped eyes full
of ancient shadow.

You're growing older
younger
than your parents did.

You pose, display what's on tap
for the night. Bog woman.
Out of your black cave
into the ragged firelight.

Now you see her, now you don't
see a woman in a bar,
drinking.

You are the retribution artist
dead rabbit in your hat,
bloodied rags up your sleeve.
Pull out
a moment of distraction, false
impressions, fake confessions,
jokes
on you.
Now you see it
now you don't,
the usual toast
just another wet defeat.

Always, a man appears
out of nowhere
lacking the gold doubloon
of his own mutiny.

He slides over, leans in,
handsome after three drinks
delightful after more.

You: up for whatever
comes after that.

You call the shots.

Feed on the Enemy

The history of your presence
                                    here
reads like a pulp novel.

In chapter one, facades fracture.
Lines are drawn, boundaries crossed
invasions reoccur. Hostages flee.
Wild times, tossed bombs, skirmishes
out of control. You wake up
with this one, that.
It will not do.
Yet it does.

When a woman is hurt
she grudge fucks
until it hurts even more.

Your war on yourself is long,
tedious, tough on the home front.
You seek leadership, find none.
A wise general would make sure
his troops fed on the enemy.
You, unwise, do the same.

The plot sickens, as do you.
Your gut roils, your poor head
jackhammers at high speed. Hands
shake with an old person's palsy.
Lies are told. Positions lost. Invaders
come and go. Come
and go.

Finally
you quit.
End of story
                    like that.

Battle scarred
you swear off the cage
that kept you in bones
you swear
you will be strong.

This lasts until it doesn't.

On the way to the gym, neon
beckons you in. Again.

You look at the row of familiar faces
wearing bodies loosely
like shrugged animal furs.
You join the hunch around the campfire.
Drink until the distance to your self
stretches, comforting you.

                         From far off
you can hear the future calling you
and it no longer matters
where you came from.

Your story begins all over
your choice a shared dream
you fall into again, not caring
your logic is bad,
your dry mouth
just a song you sing
battle hymn
for and against the self.

Him? A way
to cry out
the old war whoop
again and again.

Back to the beginning.
Again and again
it's you
alone at the bar
drinking.

To Drink or No

A new bar and you.
Fresh love. Drinks.
Stained booth in the back
by the CD jukebox.

Quarters in, music out.
Ease of transition from you—

to not you.

Reason, that old melody
does not prevail. Not here.

Piss-yellow lights dim
the dirges play
like at a drive-in
funeral home.

You distance yourself
from the gadget-addicted
fucktards, soft necks
rounded like flamingos, pink
fingers flying
through emptiness.

Warriors who win
respond to threats
in many ways,
not
with one set action.
Be prepared
when the other guy is not.
Do not go mad
with the fear
of your own nothingness.

Noise of war
in your head
muffles the search,
whoring stormtroopers
marching, marching
in your sorry skull.

You might turn out to be
your own future assassin.

You are not alone. Drinking.

A man. Another bar
another man.

You do not stop
the rounds
from coming.

Shortcomings

The local dive serves tacos
on paper plates, quivery Jell-O
shots on Friday nights.

In the bar of your choice
you must take care.
If reckless, you can be killed.
If cowardly, you may be caught.
The quick-tempered can be provoked
to rage.
A delicate humor can result
in insult. Too much
compassion may yield weakness.

                    Balance
the war sages say
while ordering
mass murders, drones, double scotches
from armchairs of leather and flesh.

And that wilderness inside you
pushing against your tender skin.

He sits down. Drinks with you.

Outside
shining and stiff, reflecting the light
                    Harleys
lined up like soldiers, waiting
for orders:

kill or be killed.

Position Yourself

At this moment you are cowering
in dark corners, glass in hand.
Hiding in full view, your uniform
cocktail waitress clothes,
escort service hairdo,
sugar baby smile.
You think you'll trap love
                         this way.

You are not alone. Drinking.

If you wish to avoid defeat—
and perhaps you do not,
you may prefer
drowning
to the fight to fill your lungs
with fresh air
                         —climb
to high ground, and turn yourself
facing the sun
                         —the sun!

Your position is bad, your head
full of twisty mazes. Dream on.

The world will not reward
your fumbling emotions. Green hills
call out your name, the echo loud
as in childhood. Your sacred objects
mount up and you hike up
the obstacle to yourself.

Stop licking old wounds.

Sunrise writes on your naked skin
tattooing your name
and the date
of your victory.

What the Enemy Wants

The night hits you hard
when the two of you leave the bar.
You are too clothed and the world
too naked.

Watch the coconut palms toss
in a sudden wind off the sea.
See the sparse scrawny pines
shiver and twist.
Trees tell you when
the enemy advances.
                                        Look:
starlings fly up, casting themselves
on the mercy of the sky: a sign
ambush is coming.

You hurry forward, rushing
to what you know will hurt
just to feel the pain
of getting it over with.

He will touch your body
all over and under your hesitancy
in his quest to feel something
not there. Not anywhere.

Park your dented Mercedes tank
across from the beach. Drink
together
from the bottle.
No chaser. No ice.

If the enemy is about to attack
you must seize something cherished
to force them
to conform
to your desires.

Take away your motivation,
your love, your attention.
Take their faith in you,
their trust, their devotion.
Remove all remnants,
leave them with nothing
of you.

There will be nothing
to attack.

You win

nothing.
Drink up.

Fire Alarm

Warlords will tell you this:
set fires at suitable times.

Tibetan monks will remind you:
attention is paid to those
who set themselves ablaze.

Isn't this what you are doing?
With him?
Drinking?
Sexing?
Letting go
of your gone
self?

You are darkness made manifest
like in monster flicks or myths.
Your face a testimony
to your self-immolation skills.
You are living somebody else's
horrible trailer-trash life.
One day at a gulp.
Your bus station loneliness
makes you smaller,
a speck
on the earth's dirty crust.

Tampered down.
Cooled.
Put out.
Your charred ruins
still smoking.

Spy in the House of Love

Now the truth comes out
along with his stiff cock.

Maybe another man
a man who maybe
meant something once
made a sort of life
with you at the core.

Where is he now
as you take the stranger
into your whiskied mouth?

Unfaithful.
Gone.

You did your part
knowing the odds.
There is no place
in this world
where espionage is not
possible. Track him down
to the ends of this filthy earth.
Focus your lens, bug his office, car,
sneak up from behind and stalk him,
eavesdrop, read his email,
texts and phone bills. Never!
Let down your guard!

                Your beloved hurts
you can be sure of that. You drink;
you can be sure of that too.
                You are the one
suffering
from a love disorder.

Tonight, yet another man
a man who cannot
give you what you lost
what you can't find
in a dick
or a glass.

Quick clouds scurry across
a black and blue sky,
suffocating stars, snuffing out
what lights your way.

You've moved on to this
to whatever happens after this.

In the uptown bar, your eyes
adjusted
roving the clamorous room
in a continuous search
for an upgrade
to your life.

There is no place
where self-hatred is not
possible. You know this
yet your cups runneth over
with hundred proof

all the proof you need
your love
                        is your ruin.

The sex is brief. He does not
ask for your number.
The hangover lasts longer
than the relationship.
Your shame longer still.

The cure for longing?
Taking pleasure
in the solitary.
You see that now?
This is the bottom of your hell
hole.
Time to climb out
of yourself.

One rung at a time. Alone.

Close your eyes and reach up
your small empty hands.

Private Room

Once, a man lay in a hospital bed
and no birds sang.
Once, a woman sat at the foot of the bed
and no dogs barked.
Once, the man's genes didn't have him up against a wall.
Night soothed.
Once, the woman was overfucked, not fucked over.
Sunlight dazzled.

Once, the man gave the woman a what for in a single malt diatribe.
Once, the man said he could make people dead and nobody laughed.
Once, the woman lived in a bus shelter and nobody cried.
Once, the man had a body like a cocked fist and no cats yowled.
Once, the woman took her punches with a smile and nobody died.
Once, the woman's smile looked like it was made with a can opener.

Once, the man loved the woman.
Birds sang. Dogs barked. Cats yowled.
Children cried.
Food tasted good. Everything tasted good.
Breezes cooled naked skin.
The weather was in a perfect mood.
The sky pearled. The globe twirled.
The sun kissed.

He insulated her bare wires.
She made his cells spark.

Nobody died.

Once, there was a difference between being something
and being something else.

Once upon a time in a hospital room
birds sang.

Amends

Behind the gritty park
in the ranky tunnels
where the local bums hung

That's where you learned
to take it
any way they'd give it to you

The booze rode shotgun
everywhere you drove
top down, strange
hands in your pants

the Irish way

In a cocktail shaker
of grace
and savagery
you survived

There are no metaphors
for it:
You survived

No hair of the dog
all the fur scraped
from your tongue

You tell us
like a bedtime story
sipping cold tea
from a stained glass.

References

Subdue the enemy without bloodshed.
Sun Tzu's *The Art of War.*

Who we are below the surface
of consciousness? What,
if anything,
does the conscious self decide?
AJ Adams's *Undrunk: A Skeptic's Guide to AA.*

Alcohol leads to predictability.
John O'Brien's *Leaving Las Vegas.*

Incentives that channel
your greed. Your thirst.
Caroline Knapp's *Drinking, a Love Story.*

Sipping life like a dry martini,
smashing the glass in the fireplace
of your future.
Mary Karr's *Lit.*

Face like a grandfather
clock, face like a time
bomb, face that testifies
to drinking valor, loss.
Charles Bukowski:
anything, everything.

about the author: a poem

sober, sober, sober
drunk a little
sober
sober
sober
drunk a little more
sober
drunk too much
sober
drunk
drunk one last time
sober, sober, sober
sober
drinking a little
sober
not drinking
sober
writing about drinking
writing about not drinking
sober
sober, sober, so...

Mickey J. **Corrigan** is a drunken reverie, a fluke of the imagination, an avatar who works as a pulp fiction writer, bar girl, and nonsense gatherer. She lives in South Florida, where the men run guns and the women run after them. War is constantly on everyone's mind—personal wars, private wars, income generating wars. But so is love, with a chaser of anonymous sex. And drink, oh yes. Poetry is not. But then, it's all just one big war-torn lovelorn drunken poem, isn't it?

Mickey's novellas and novels have been published by a variety of independent presses in the US, UK, Canada, and Australia. In 2017, Salt Publishing in the UK will release her neo-noir crime novel *Project XX*.

Check out more of Mickey's lucid dreams at www.mickeyjcorrigan. com or on Tumblr: http://mickeyjcorrigan.tumblr.com.

CPSIA information can be obtained
at www.ICGtesting.com
Printed in the USA
LVOW12s0402141216
517205LV00001B/27/P